God Did Something Good When Something Bad Was Happening

Kinsley Reed

Love Clones Publishing
www.lcpublishing.net

Copyright © 2015 by Kinsley Reed. All rights reserved. This book or any portion thereof may not be reproduced or used in any manner whatsoever without the express written permission of the publisher except for the use of brief quotations in a book review.

Printed in the United States of America

First Printing, 2015

ISBN: 978-0692577936

King James Version Scripture quotations marked "KJV" are taken from the Holy Bible, King James Version (Public Domain).

Publishers:
Love Clones Publishing
Chicago, IL 60604
www.lcpublishing.net

Dedication

This book is dedicated in the memory of my beloved mother Mrs. La'Gayla Sonta Smalls-Reed who became my angel on October 11, 2011. I know she is watching over me every day.

Mommy I miss you and I know you are happy to see me going on with my life while keeping your legacy alive through me. I know you are also proud of me for writing my first book. Mommy, God truly has done something good when something bad happened in my life.

I love you Mommy and I dedicate my first book to you.

Acknowledgements

First, I would like to give honor to God and I thank Him for being there for me when I needed Him the most.

To my parents La'Gayla "Sonta" Smalls-Reed and Fred Reed for bringing me into this world and making me the person I am today.

To my grandparents who have always been there for me and always encouraged me to be the best in everything I do. Love you much.

To my two older sisters Imani and Karrington I'm so glad God gave me big sisters like you. Even though y'all always pick at me, I love you very much and I'm always praying for you as YOUR OVERSEER.

To my Family, my aunts, my uncles, my cousins, and my friends, thank you for always supporting and caring for me. God bless each of you. I Love you.

I would like to give a special thank you and honor to Pastor Tonya McQuire for helping me a lot on this book and for being an awesome lady in my life. I Love you Pastor T.

To my best friend Kailtyn L. Bodison thank you for being my bestie and for always being there for me. I Love you.

To My Friend Asherah Murphy I thank God for allowing us to be friends and I look forward to many more years as your friend.

I want to give special honor to a very important person in my life, my Uncle Elder S.M Ricey Reed. Thank you Uncle Ricey for teaching me how to live Godly. I Love you.

To everyone who reads this book thank you for your support, God bless each of you.

Love,
Kinsley Reed

TABLE OF CONTENTS

Introduction

Chapter 1
Called From My Mother's Womb

Chapter 2
Mother's Last Words To Me

Chapter 3
Moving Forward

Chapter 4
Hearing The Word From God

Chapter 5
Some Will Not Believe You Are Real

Chapter 6
Trials and Tribulations

Chapter 7
Something Good Was About to Happen

Chapter 8
I'm Growing Up

Chapter 9
Memories Live Forever

INTRODUCTION

On October 11, 2011, our day as a family went pretty normal. My sisters, Imani, Karrington and I went to school as we did each day. That afternoon we had fun after dinner and we went to bed, not knowing that later on that night our lives would change so quickly and so unexpectedly.

On this dreaded night 4 years ago my mother La'Gayla Sonta Smalls-Reed died suddenly from a blood clot in her lungs. The person I knew I could always count on was no longer with me and I was only six years old.

I didn't know that evening when she fixed my hair for school pictures the next day and she kissed me, said good night, and said I love you, that would be the last time I would hear my mommy's voice, feel my mommy's touch and see my mommy face to face. What was I going to do? Who's going to fix my hair pretty when I had school pictures? Who's going to help me with my homework? Who's going to help me get my bath? Who's going to tuck me in bed and read my bedtime story? Who? Mommy isn't here to do these things for me anymore.

I never knew such pain and a lot of it I didn't even understand but I had a strong family that prayed for me and with me.

God inspired me to write, "God Did Something Good When Something Bad Was Happening" because I told Him I wanted to help other kids who had loss their mommy or daddy. I know this book will help others to keep moving forward and to know that they will make it.

As I share my life with you, I ask you for your prayers, I want God to be happy with me and get the glory out of my life. One day I will see my Mother again, for *God Did Something Good, When Something Bad Was Happening*!

I hope you enjoy this book as much as I have enjoyed writing it.

CHAPTER 1
Called From My Mother's Womb

On July 29, 2005, in the Colleton Medical Center, Walterboro, SC, a beautiful bouncy baby girl was born to Fred and Sonta Reed. They proudly named this beautiful bundle of joy Kinsley Alexandria Reed. What mommy and daddy didn't realize that day was that they were holding in their arms one of God's chosen ones. Jeremiah 1:5 says "Before I formed you in the belly I knew you and before you came forth out of your mother's womb, I sanctified you, and I ordained you a prophet unto the nations.

I have always had a love for church and I enjoy going and I love giving God praise. When I was around three I began to tell my parents that I was going to be an Evangelist, telling everyone about the goodness of God and about His grace. My Mother would always smile and say " Alright Kinsley". What I didn't know was my faith in God would be put to the test at such an early age. I was so young when my mommy died and not as strong in the Lord as an adult, but I've learned that God does not put more on us then we can bear. God knew me before I knew myself and He knew his plans for my life. Since God doesn't have a respect of persons I too face trials and tribulations, like an adult, but He's given me the strength to endure. Some things in my life, even at an early age remain a mystery to me. I've come to realize that as long as we live, we will never have a full answer to all that happens in life, but we must trust God. God knows everything about each and everyone of us. It's amazing to know that God knew what was going to happen to my family and me before we even knew it. He knew that he was going to put my mother here on this earth, let her meet and marry my Daddy, then he was going to bless her to have me, Kinsley, His prophet to the Nations. What I have learned is when things happen God is not surprised. What I did not know, what my daddy did not know, what my sisters, grandparents and uncles did not know is that God only put my Mother on this earth for 39 years and on October 11, 2011 he was going to call her to heaven to be with Him.

The Bible says when you know God and are no longer in your body you are with God. Even though my Mother isn't here with us today, we know that she's in heaven with the Lord and He's given us a guardian heavenly angel to watch over us. We didn't know that something bad would happen in our life and our whole world would suddenly be turned upside down, but God knew and He knew we would get through it. Everyday He makes us stronger and we can move forward even when this unexpected situation happened to us.

Chapter 2
Mother's Last Words

My sisters and I did not know that on that dreadful Tuesday night when our mother told us good night, she loved us and that we needed to go to bed because we had an early morning tomorrow, that would be the last time we would hear her voice, embrace our Mother with a hug and feel our mother's arms around us. We really didn't know that we would wake up the next morning and our Mother would be gone forever!

I was so sad, hurt, lonely and afraid I was only six years old and now I would never see my Mommy again. I was so scared because I didn't know what my sisters and I were going to do without our Mother. I just didn't know. I didn't know what my Daddy was going to do without his wife, what my grandparents were going to do without their daughter and what my uncles were going to do without their sister. Truly our world was shaken apart very quickly. How could something good come out of something this bad?

"For I know the thoughts that I think toward you, saith the LORD, thoughts of peace, and not of evil, to give you an expected end." Jeremiah 29:11 (KJV)

We didn't know what we were going to do, but God knew what His plans were for the Reed Family even when we didn't. It was during this time that we had to rely on God even the more and trust that He really did have a plan for us and it was not a plan to hurt or harm us.

All of our family and friends came to our home after Mommy left us. Even everyone from my school, where my Mother was the guidance counselor, came to be with us during this time, but we were still so sad, hurt, and confused. As the days passed I was more scared because I didn't know what to do. My Daddy was always crying for my Mother. We all wanted her to come back to us, but it didn't happen and only God knew why. We had to live without her and there was nothing that my family could do about it.

Our Mother was gone to be an angel with the Lord. At first I didn't know what an angel was because that night when my Daddy told my sisters and I that our Mother was gone to be an angel now, I remember asking him "What is an Angel". My daddy tearfully said, "Why us?" and I remembered at the age of six, hugging my daddy and saying, "You have to stop crying, you have to be here for us and we are going to make it."

Two weeks after my mother died, I received the Superintendent List Award and I remembered before I went to bed that night my Mother died she was checking over some school work that I had done and I missed two of the problems on the worksheet and she told me that she wanted me to always pay attention and take my time so I wouldn't make any more careless mistakes, because she knew that I knew the lesson, but I was not paying attention. My parents and grandparents always instilled good manners and the importance of getting good grades in school to my sisters and me. We always made the Superintendent List, the Principal's List and Honor Roll in school.

My sisters and me promised that we would keep our Mother's legacy alive by getting the best education that we possibly can and would always work hard in school and do our best. With my Daddy, grandparents and family I have no choice but to do just that because Mommy always said there is no failure in us.

My desire and calling for my life is to be a doctor as well as an Evangelist for the Kingdom of God. I always told my Mother that

I wanted to be an evangelist and preach God's word and she always encouraged me and told me I could be whatever I wanted to be. I know that I want to take care of the body and soul of the people of God. I have a great love and concern for the people of God, especially young people.

I know that in order for me to be a good doctor, I must get a good education, so my Mother's last words to me will always be with me and will be my encouragement on those days when I feel weary in pursuit of my career. I will keep my Mother's legacy alive by dedicating myself to my school and studies to become a successful doctor and Evangelist because I know that's what God has called me to do.

Chapter 3
Moving Forward - Philippians 3:14

After my mommy died, my grandparents along with Uncle Ricey moved in with us. At that time, I have watched my Uncle Ricey as a minister and my grandfather, Franklin Smalls as a Lay Speaker minister to God's people. From watching them I developed a desire to go into the ministry.

In the past, my house was Christian based, but it was not the main point. Our home was primarily filled with educational goals, but now I am being blessed with having my dad instill educational and spiritual goals in the home. During this time, I began to bond with my uncle. Asking questions and as he would say becoming a "bugga-boo". He began to study the bible with me everyday. As time went on, I began to enjoy watching the WORD network. One of my favorite pastors that I enjoy watching is Pastor Kimberly Ray. Through the spiritual presence that lies within our home, I see a difference in our family with my daddy and my sisters. My daddy once owned very popular nightclubs within Walterboro, SC and surrounding areas. The funniest thing that I've learned growing up is my daddy and Uncle Ricey are 10 years apart in age and they both think differently. My daddy often says he was building the devil's kingdom while Uncle Ricey was building God's kingdom, but now my daddy's mission is to spread the gospel through his marketplace ministry. He decided to establish the LSR Enterprise in honor of my mother's memory. Now I see two powerful men that are very important in my life working alongside each other with God's Blessings and they are moving LSR Enterprise forward. The purpose of LSR Enterprise is to help someone else as they go through life, to accomplish some of the things that they may have thought that they could never obtain, like home ownership, business owners, musical careers and to help with college. Yes! Something good can happen out of something bad, God made it happen!

There were many voids that were placed in my life. No one could ever replace my mother, but now I have multiple people stepping in. It has brought us closer together as a family. Even my PaPa stays with us now to cook our favorite meals and I must say my favorite is sausage, rice and pork & beans, yes!

We have now moved into a larger home where all the family can come together and we have so much fun! The questions that I once had, "Who will bathe me?" "Who will fix my hair?" "Who will help me with my homework?" Now I can take my pick, because I have several people that can help me. Yes, something good can come out of something bad.

Chapter 4
Hearing The Call From God...

The months after my Mother died were really hard on my family and me. My Uncle Ricey would bring us together and pray with us when we wake up, on our way to school and at night. It seemed like the more we prayed, the more afraid I was becoming. It seemed like the more we prayed for God to help us through this trying time, the more my daddy would cry every night for my mother. It was really hard going through this especially seeing my daddy cry for mom.

One day, as we, my uncle, grandmother and me, were walking through our house praying and rebuking the spirit of grief, I heard a voice say, "Pray in the Holy Ghost, pray in the Holy Ghost", and that was when my prayer life really began.

On Wednesdays our Youth Ministry meets

and I couldn't wait to get to the Elder Mazie Moultrie Memorial Youth Center on those days because it gave me strength and it was there when I began to speak to young people, telling them about the goodness of God and how God can make something good come out of something bad when it happens to us. I also talked with them about the importance of a good education and the need to make good grades and to obey those that have rule over you.

I've always been taught that good behavior is just as important as having good grades. For God wants us to act like children, because we are not an adult, and that we must listen and obey the rules that's set for us in our homes, in our schools, in our church and community.

It wasn't long after that I was being asked to speak on various youth services at churches and youth programs. I also have the honor of being the Co-Host of the radio program called

The Reflections Of Hope Show every Sunday and I travel all over the Low-Country with my Uncle, Elder S.M. Ricey Reed, as well with my Dance Ministry of The Progressive Church of Jesus.

I know that God will help me to overcome every trying time, every trial and situation as long as I continue to praise Him. I know when I am sad, a dance and a praise will make me glad.

Chapter 5
Some Will Not Believe You Are Real

As I began to travel along with my Uncle Ricey in the ministry, some people laughed at me, some didn't believe that I was for real, when I said that God has called me to be an Evangelist to go telling of His goodness. Even my sisters Imani and Karrington, especially Karrington, teased me and called me a fake Evangelist, but I kept going forth because I know God called me to be His mouthpiece. Even though I was afraid and at times ashamed because of the teasing from my peers, I kept the faith and as my Uncle continued to encourage and teach me the way of Holiness, just like my great-grandmother taught him, I began to grow in the Lord.

Sometimes, I was ashamed to tell my friends at school that I wanted to be a preacher, but my Uncle Ricey and my Grandmother told me to never disown God. The Bible says in Romans 1:16 "I am not ashamed of the gospel of Christ for it is the power of God unto salvation to everyone that believeth.

So I knew that I couldn't be ashamed of spreading the Word of God, as time went on I began to stand for the gospel of Jesus Christ. My sisters finally admitted to me that they believed in me and they would support me, but they just liked to tease me because I let it get under my skin and they just wanted to upset me.

When I heard the message that God gave my Uncle Ricey to preach one Sunday and it was "Don't let the devil see you sweat." I immediately stopped letting everything someone said about me not being a real Evangelist get me so upset. Moms Grandma Reed said "Just pray for them Kinsley", and I did.

Chapter 6
Trials and Tribulations

Hebrew 13:5 says that God promises to never leave me nor forsake me. At the age of six I lost my mother to a pulmonary embolism, which is a blood clot to the lung. My grandfather Smalls had open-heart surgery and multiple strokes. My grandmother Reed had knee replacement. My PaPa Reed had multiple blocked arteries in which stints were inserted to support his heart. My Uncle Greg lost his eyesight from a disease that is common among twins and recently had surgery due to swelling on his brain which caused him to have seizures. My spiritual mentor, Uncle Ricey is battling cancer. These are things as a ten year old that I live with daily.

As if all of this was not enough, I was diagnosed with scoliosis. I had a fifty degree spinal curve that required surgery. October 13,

2015, I was in surgery for over six hours, which required the doctors to cut my back to insert two metal rods and twenty screws in my spine. I was hospitalized for five days. I have to engage in six weeks of rehabilitation in order to heal completely. During my hospital visit, I experience physical pain that I had never experienced in my life. I had to take some of the same medicines my Uncle Ricey was given during his chemotherapy treatments. I had to take morphine steadily through my IV along with hydrocodone for pain. I also had to learn to walk again. I have to adjust my life now with metal rods in my back. I cannot do what "normal" kids can do. I can only imagine during this surgery, my mom would have been right by my side. I felt her presence there telling me that everything is going to be okay. While I was in the hospital, those voids that I spoke of earlier were filled. My daddy never left my side. Other family members supported me. They helped me. They waited on me because I loved to be waited on. Someone was always there to lend a helping hand, and my PaPa even cooked my favorite meal and brought it to the hospital for me to eat. Everyone from my school was great also.

After the doctors released me, that support travelled to my home as I began my rehabilitation. My cousin would personally come fix my hair. My 5th grade teacher became my homebound teacher. I constantly had the support of my sisters and my family. There is a large age difference between my sisters and me. I am the baby girl. They are closer in age. Therefore, they are very good friends. My sisters are very tough on me at times, but they have helped me a lot in my rehabilitation. This crisis made us become much closer. My dad continues to support and provide for our family. I also feel that our bond has strengthened in this situation. I know that my dad will always be there for me.

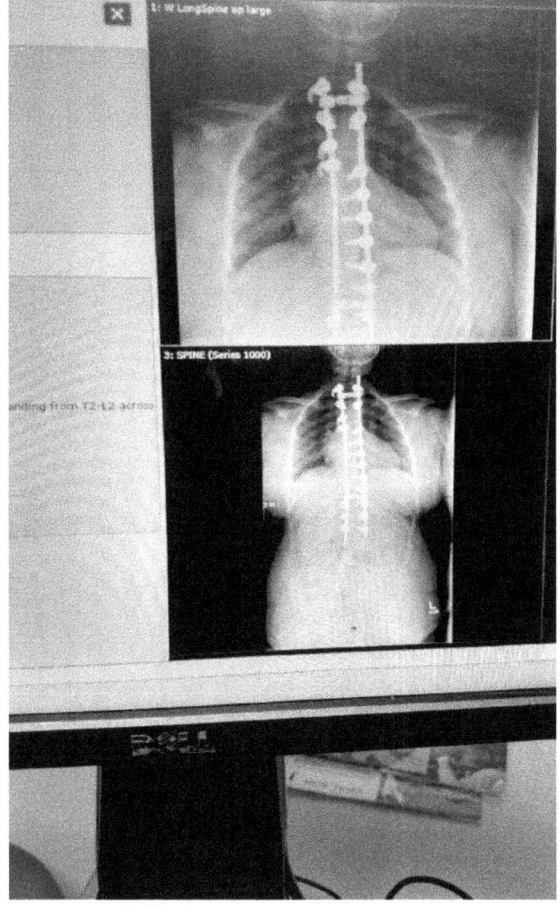

Chapter 7
Something Good was about to Happen

Several years have passed now since my Mother went to be with the Lord and the spirit of fear is not as forceful upon me as it used to be when she first left us, but I was not completely delivered concerning losing my Mother at an early age.

I remember one Saturday afternoon our Dance Ministry from Progressive Church had a program called "Praise In Advance" I had a solo part in our last dance selection called "The Blood Still Works" and as I begin to dance, I turned around and I saw a form that looked like my Mother, just smiling at me with her arms opened wide, just like the picture that's on this book.

I started to stop dancing and cry, but she shook her head as if to say Go Kinsley Go! I really began to praise God in the dance for yes

I know that the blood of Jesus had me and my family covered. That no hurt, harm or danger would come upon us why, because the blood still works! I also know it will never lose its power. Hallelujah! Every since that day, the spirit of fear began to leave me, for the memories of my Mother will forever live inside of my heart.

Anytime I am nervous or afraid of doing something, I can hear her voice say, "Go Kinsley Go"! And when I am lonely and sad, she will be with me in the spirit. For I can do all things through Christ Jesus that strengthens me! Why? Because I am covered with the blood of Jesus, and the blood still works! Yes! Something good is coming out of a bad situation.

Chapter 8
I'm Growing Up

As I grow, from year to year, so many good things and so many bad things have happened to my family and me. But one good thing is that my family has stayed together and like Uncle Ricey always says "A family that prays together, stays together" and boy do we pray. Every morning after Grandma Reed gets me ready for school, I go into my Daddy's room and we pray together.

When we get into the car and Uncle Ricey takes us to school he leads my sisters and I into prayer and he has each one of us pray. Sometimes we pray all the way to school. We say, "Please Uncle Ricey do we have to pray all the way to school" but that's just like my Uncle Ricey he keep us lifted before the Lord. He loves the Lord and He loves his family. He knows what prayer can do because he is a cancer survivor.

Our Family has been touched with trials and tribulations. My Mother died at a young age, my Daddy is a diabetic, my grandfathers have heart trouble, my grandmother has several health issues and now I am faced with a serious spinal condition and had to have a major back surgery at the age of 10 years old, but I know when something bad is happening God is able to make something good happen out of it.

I know that my praise and my prayer life have helped me to make it this far along with hope and determination. The older I get and the more time I spend in prayer I feel stronger and I have a closer relationship with God.

A relationship with God is just like the good friendship I have with my friend Kait. We have been best friends for a long time and the more we talk and play together, the closer that we become as friends.

That's what you have to do to have a close relationship with God, you have to talk to him in prayer and you have to know him by reading and studying His word.

Sometimes I may forget to do it, but I am trying to remember to spend a certain amount of time each day, talking to God in prayer and reading His Word. The Bible is so important because it is the Word of God and it teaches us what God desires for us to do. The Bible teaches us how we are supposed to treat each other, how we are suppose to live and how we are suppose to grow stronger in him.

When I do what God says for me to do, when I give the Lord all of me, than I will have the blessed assurance of seeing my Mother again. Oh how I want to see my Mother again to look into her sweet face, to see her beautiful smile and to hear her say to me, "Go Kinsley Go, You can do this... This is my baby, The Evangelist."

Chapter 9
Memories Live Forever

Even though my Mother is gone, and she will never be here with us in the flesh, her spirit is with us everyday, and we can keep her legacy alive through us.

My Mother was a great educator and worked in Colleton County School District for many years. She was a Guidance Counselor at Forest Hills Elementary School and she strived daily for every child to receive a good education.

She loved and worked hard for every student at Forest Hill not just my sisters and me. They have installed a monument in front of the school in memory of my Mother, La'Gayla Sonta Smalls-Reed.

Soon after my mother's death, the Lord laid it on my daddy's heart to start a scholarship fund for deserving seniors who desire to get a college degree. For the past four years, we have been having the La'Gayla Sonta Smalls Reed benefit concert with famous and local gospel artist. My daddy also started LSR Media Group, which helps local artist to achieve their dreams as a gospel singer, because my Mother loved gospel singing.

God has been blessing LSR Enterprise and we have traveled all over the LowCountry and have also traveled to the Stellar Awards in Las Vegas. To God be the glory! Something good is coming out of something bad because my Daddy is allowing my mother's legacy to live through us as we keep her dream and willingness to help others alive every day in LSR Enterprise.

Through all of this we know God holds the keys to your future, because when the devil says no about our lives, God will say yes! With God, you can have that home, that career, that business, you can write a book or get that college education because dreams do come true, if we let them. Just remember, just like my Mother told me, "You can do this Kinsley, Go For It" and I got myself together and begin to dance for the glory of God!

I am so grateful to have such a wonderful father that is willing to listen and do what I ask him to do. My Daddy will do just about anything that me and my sisters ask him to do. Even when some of the things we ask for cost a lot of money.

I went to my Daddy and I told him that I wanted to write a book about my life like Uncle Ricey was going to do, and he said, "Are you sure about this Kinsley?" And I said, "Yes Daddy, I want to do this". Since my daddy is the great Dad that he is my dream has come true. Yes, good things can come out of something that is bad!

Daddy I love you and I thank God for you and one day we will see Momma again.

MY ACCOMPLISHMENTS

2011 – Supt. List

2012 – Honor Roll

2013 – Supt List

2014 – Honor Roll

2015 – Supt List

Prayze Factor People Choice Awards- Atlanta, GA

Youth on the Rise
Academic Achievement Award

For I know that my family is under the precious blood of Jesus, and yes the Blood still works for it will never lose its power.

For the past 4 years, God has use me and anointed me as a Prayer Warrior to pray for our family, so that the spirit of grief will not destroy us. I have seen God move! We will never get over the loss of our Mother but God is helping us accept the things we can't change and the wisdom to know the difference.

Pray for me as I go forth in God.

ABOUT THE AUTHOR

Kinsley Alexandra Reed is the daughter of Mr. Fred A and the Late La'Gayla Sonta Reed of Walterboro, SC.

She is a 5th grader at Forest Hill Elementary. She's an A+ and Superintendent Honor Roll Student. She's an active member of Progressive Church of Jesus-Walterboro, SC where she serves on the Praise Dance Ministry and as a Youth Ministry Leader.

For Booking:
Contact Tonya McQuire 843-217-2664
Email: angelswic@yahoo.com

Fred Reed 843-908-2023
Email: fredreed91@aol.com

Follow Kinsley on Facebook @ EvangelistKinsley

www.ingramcontent.com/pod-product-compliance
Lightning Source LLC
Chambersburg PA
CBHW072040060426
42449CB00010BA/2371